thou
shalt
not
fear

thou shalt not fear

Bud Collyer

fleming h. revell company

To Marian
who listened so lovingly
and criticized so gently;
   and
the Reverend C. John L. Bates, Jr.
who first inspired
and then encouraged.

ðeðication

Actually, this did not start out to be a book at all. I began writing sermons in verse for some lay preaching I am occasionally invited to do, and here are a few of them.

It is a collection (and a small one at that!) of sermons, each of which, in turn, is a collection of thoughts and ideas which passed through my mind while listening to good preachers preach, while teaching my Sunday school class, or while talking with God.

If anything said herein causes anyone to become more acutely aware of the ever-present power of the love of God, then the collecting will not have been in vain.

BUD COLLYER

preface

contents

thou shalt not fear

What can we do to wipe away those fears
That strive so hard to claim us for their own?
What can we do when walking through the years
To make us know none goes his way alone?

A New York Corporation advertises
That it has many shapes and many sizes,
Some concrete and some steel, some underground,
Some that are square and some
        that are quite round,
All equally protective for the day
The nuclear bomb should chance to come our way.
They'll build it for you—one room,
        two or three—
Depending on the size, the cost will be
From high to inexpensive, all depending
On just how much you think
        you should be spending!

11

How scared are you? How frightened?
        How much fear
Both for yourself and those you hold most dear?
Or just how big a bomb do you expect?
Figure out these answers! They'll erect
The shelter that will do the most for you!
The shelter that will really see you through!

Once upon a long, long time ago
I donned a bathing suit and water wings
To learn the art of swimming. Even though
I longed to learn to do the many things
The other boys were doing in the lake—
The backstroke, sidestroke, breaststroke,
        and the crawl—
I realized the courage it would take
For me to learn. I even tried to stall
And put it off! But friends took me in hand
And led me to the water's edge. I sat
And slowly inched my way. I couldn't stand!
If I had tried I would have fallen flat
Upon my face! But finally my feet
Made contact with the water—then my knees!
When finally immersion was complete

12

I floated as serenely as you please!
With water wings well filled with air, why not?
In the ensuing long and tedious days
I managed to accomplish quite a lot
In learning all the many different ways
To stay afloat, to swim, and then to dive.
I learned to save a life and stay alive!
I learned to swim so well within that year!
And above all I learned to have no fear!

When God made man a cut above the rest
Of all creation, he was well endowed
With all the attributes that made him best
Above all creatures, and he was allowed
A full, free choice of will to chart his course
In any way his slightest whim might choose;
Free to use intelligence or force,
Free to win a battle or to lose!
His is a mighty heritage indeed,
To look around among his friends and foes,
Selecting allies for his every need,
Marshaling all his strength before he throws
The gauntlet in the path or in the face
Of any other one who might oppose!

Free to win honor or to bring disgrace
To those who trust in him, whose voices rose
In cheers and battle cries when it began,
Beyond the credibility of man!
If victory is his, he is a hero!
If overcome, his courage reaches zero!
When facing loss of all he holds most dear
Man, for the first time, knows
        the chill of fear!
That small, four-letter word which paralyzes
The mind, and makes the heart to beat too fast,
And makes man stop before he realizes
He's not the first, nor will he be the last
To know the bitter pain of indecision
Causing those who used to cheer to laugh,
To face his every outburst with derision
And cut his every confidence in half
Before it falls entirely away
And leaves him standing naked, while the crowd
Tramples on the earth where he held sway!
Can he then stand erect, his head unbowed
By threats of retribution if he seeks
To ferret out the faith which he once knew?
It may take minutes, hours, days, or weeks,

Or even years for love to struggle through
Before man takes his God down from the shelf
And learns to love another as himself!

Meanwhile, what course of action should we take
When fear knocks at our doors?
        What can we say?
How will we find the fortitude to shake
The paralyzing bonds of fear away?
I've heard it said, when fear
        knocks at the door
Send faith to answer it, and you will find
That there is no one there; and what is more
That we are all particularly blind,
For faith is always there for you and me,
It's just our own unwillingness to see!

The lights are burning mighty late these days
To chase the shadows from the laboratories,
As scientists discover all the ways
To help us put an end to all our worries
With instant death! It comes in many sizes
With many different names! It advertises
If you'll just put your trust in God aside

And let the manufacturer provide
Some powdered faith to spread upon your bread
You'll love their product—
            even though you're dead!
Just think of all the man-hours spent today
In dreaming up new measures of destruction!
If we should take one twenty-fifth away
And concentrate it on a new construction
Of love and deep concern for all mankind,
Regardless of the color, race, or creed,
With just that tiny effort we would find
That we can use our every thought and deed
In building for the Lord our God! We'd see
His blueprints clearly showing how to build
The right kind of a life for you and me;
A life of action, every moment filled
With things to do for others! Every line
Will show the way so clearly no mistakes,
No errors can be made, save yours and mine
If we should trust our future to the fakes,
The charlatans, inhabiters of Hell
Who try to make us join the growing band
By shouting, "Come on in, the fire's swell!
This is a real hot buy! The Promised Land

Is nothing but a promise! Settle here!
We'll build to suit! Just tell us your desire!
Our price is not too cheap, but not too dear!
We build with Grade-A brimstone! Take a flier!"

God is a quiet builder. All creation
Attests to this. And when the Lord God looks
And sees that it is good, then every nation
That seeks to write its name in history books
Must know this is the building each must buy
To mount a wakeful watch and be secure
In knowing it shall live and never die,
In knowing young and old and rich and poor
Stand before Jesus in the selfsame light
That led Him down the throughway to the cross,
That ended for all time the dark of night
By light of truth! It seemed like such a loss
To those who walked with Him, to whom He said,
"O ye of little faith! Your Father knows
Your needs! Why are ye fearful? Do not dread
The storms of life! Stand up against the blows,
O ye of little faith!"
                                    Stand up with God!
And find out what it is to know no fear.

No matter what the cost, the very sod
On which you stand may bring a price so dear
That wealth in all its reaches may not bring
Such peace of heart that makes
 the soul to sing!

The Psalmist one time said, "Except the Lord
Build the house, the workers build in vain!"
If you would be secure, no truer word
Was ever said; and in the Psalms again,
"Unless the Lord watches over the city
The watchman stays awake in vain!"
        A pity
So many of us try to build alone
And end up with a heartless mound of stone!
Banish all uncertainty! Be sure
And you will be secure! Don't let the fear
That grips the world and makes it insecure
Keep you in torment! God has made it clear
So many times, Old Testament and New,
Time and again: "Fear not! Fear not!
 Fear not!"
Too bad so many fear! Too bad so few
Can recognize God's hand before the rot

Begins to undermine the walls of truth
With lies and self-deceptions, until fright
Even claims the stalwart hearts of youth
And makes of every day a dreadful night!
Is this what you want?
          To be a scare-scarred soul?
Are you convinced that everything is lost?
Then read the ad and have them dig the hole
And hide in it, no matter what the cost!
Remembering, though you dig
          with might and main,
Unless the Lord God digs, you dig in vain!

Where shall we put our faith
          these troubled days
With all the frightened talk
          that fills the air?
How shall we find the way to mend our ways?
How can we find the calm that seems so rare?
Read the ad again! Read it at length!
Then hear the Psalmist calling
          through the rubble,
"God is still our refuge and our strength,
Our only very present help in trouble!"

We've come to pretty passes in our time
But none to match the one we're in today
Which sees us blinded by the dust and grime
Of insecurity and fear! Our way
To that bright goal we called our destiny,
To lead all men to freedom and to love,
Seems to be blocked, because we will not see
The light that shines so brightly from above,
Steady and strong and piercing
        through the clouds
Which Communism uses to confuse
And to confound the frightened,
        brain-washed crowds
Who only seek a doctrine they can use
To bring some order to their headlong flight
Out of confusion to eternal night!
But we can, *if we will,* so clearly see
The light beyond, over, above the dark,
Which breaks through every bond
        and sets men free!
And even where the Reds have made their mark
Across the freedom of the human race
There is a price once paid
        for all men's souls—

Completely paid in full—it can erase
All scars of evil, meanwhile heaping coals
Upon the heads of lying, shameless men
Who strut across the earth and seek to smash
Whatever liberty remains, and then
Smile while the last free fires burn to ash!
But don't forget—some smiled
        when Jesus died!
Some washed their hands of it;
        some turned away.
Some stared, some wept,
        and still some others tried
Pretending what had taken place that day
Had never really happened. But it did!
And left behind a brilliant light to shine
And lead men out of darkness! God forbid
That we should ever have to fall in line
And stand for hours, waiting for our turn
To gaze upon a corpse entombed in glass,
Worshiping mortal man's remains and earn
The praise of fellow workers as we pass!
Are we afraid of people such as this,
Who hammer out their sickly lies and seek
To conquer all men with a Judas kiss

While the Red earth inherits all the meek?
Think hard on your inheritance! Think hard!
We have no glass-cased body to observe!
We have the living Jesus Christ, the Lord!
We have His living presence! If we swerve
Too far to left or right, He'll bring us back
And keep us on the straight and narrow track
That brings us to the place that knows no fear,
The presence of our God who holds us dear!
What is your desire? Take your choice!
Fear of something powerless and dead,
Whose only force comes from a lying voice
Seeking to still the truth, and in its stead
Implant the lie! Is this what you prefer?
Or faith in One whom man could not inter,
Whose power is the everlasting love
In which He holds us all, whose very death
Proved that His power came from God above
In rising from the grave and taking breath
In mortal life again, that we might see
Ours is a mission in eternity
To wipe all fears away, that we might be
Free, in the gospel that sets all men free!

Through all the noise of traffic,
        through the din
Of all the clamor for material gain
Through all the gloss of masquerading sin
Comes Jesus' invitation, clear and plain,
In simple words that all may understand
In troubled times,
        when flames of hate are fanned,—
So quietly, yet loud enough to hear,
And to each human heart it has to say:
"Fear not, for I am with you all—alway!"

You've got the invitation! Do you see
Down at the very bottom of the card
The usual request: "R. S. V. P."?
Will you respond to Jesus? Is it hard
To make your mind up? Is it hard to think
Of just the thing to say? You didn't know
You'd have to answer? Were you on the brink
Of putting it aside, to let it go?
There cannot be a meeting of the minds,
Divine mind and the human mind, unless
When God says He's with us, He also finds

That *we're* with *Him!* Unless we each confess:
"I'm with you, God! In all ways, *I'm* with *you!*"
"What must be done, God? Here I am! Send
    me!"
"Help me to speak the truth that sets men free!"
The swamplands and the marshes will not float
Around you as you stand still in your track.
The time comes when you have to take a boat
And lean into the oars and put your back
In every stroke, until you once again
Float free and see again the distant shore
Which you will one day reach and feel the pain
That tells you that you live to die no more!
I pray that we may live to see the day
When we hear Jesus call along the way:
"Fear not, for I am with you!" And we'll say:
"We're with you, too, dear Jesus, all the way!"

Remember the old game of "Put and Take"?
Let's play it once again for Jesus' sake!
Remember you must "put" before you "take"
The future of our world to be the stake!
Remember to be loved you must first love
Another as yourself, or life will be

24

All empty days of fear which never move
And never make much sense for you and me.
Remember to be hated you must hate!
Such poison as can fill the human brain
Seems to make a mockery of fate
And turn the wheels of warfare once again!
Remember to be served you must first serve!
First reach into a life that's not your own,
Bring warmth and comfort to a shattered nerve—
You'll know the love that never lives alone!
Remember you must give before you get!
Give freely of yourself when there is need!
Follow Jesus everywhere; and yet
Where there are cowards, be prepared to lead!
Remember you must seek before you find
All that there is in life worth looking for
Which brings the love of heart
    and soul and mind
Which knows and fills our every need and more!
Remember, *put* your faith in God, and *take*
The only stand to lead the world to peace—
Stand steadfast as a Christian
    for Christ's sake!
And hate and greed and sin and war must cease!

25

Have faith in God! Do not have faith in fear!
Add this commandment to the list of ten!
Let the commandment be: "Thou shalt not fear!"
And when you've said it once, say it again!
"Fear not, for I am with you!" saith the Lord.
What better place for faith than in God's Word?
Christ died and rose again to make it clear
To all men of all times: "Thou shalt not fear!"

what would we do?

If we all knew that each of us must die
Within the hour, just what would we do?
And while you think about it, I shall try
To do my best to make quite clear to you
Just why I posed a question such as this,
Supposing Death has aimed and cannot miss!
Now mind you, I don't want a violent death
For any one of us. I simply mean
That if we knew we'd soon draw our last breath
Within the hour, with scant time between
To clean the house and set the record straight,
To put aside the many childish things,
Look squarely at ourselves and clean the slate
Before we stand and face the King of kings,
What would we do?
     Each one of us must know
That once upon a happy long ago
God made us—though our loving Mothers bore us,

Fed us, loved us, rocked us to and fro
As every night we joined the age-old chorus
Which was our way of first communicating
That we had put a damper on her life.
She tried to sleep, and as we lay there, waiting
To get our change, we made life damper still,
With tears, I mean! We kept it up until
Pop wondered what had happened to his wife!
How could she sleep so soundly while we cried,
And be so wide awake each time he tried
To sneak in from an evening with the boys?
He lost a lot of sleep, and so did she!
If they protested loudly, so did we!
But it was not all hardship; there were joys
Too numerous to mention; times of pleasures
That somehow always seemed to counteract
Those other times when we were less
        than treasures!
We made the most of everything! In fact,
We learned too soon that there were other ways
Of honoring our father and our mother
Than just the way the old commandment says!
A smile! A hug! A kiss! And many other
Artifices we'd all recognize

If we could take the time to list them all;
The way we'd open up our big blue eyes
Each time we tried to tell the story tall!
Each "don't" became the thing we had to do,
Each "stop" a thing we simply must go through!
And each parental warning soon became
A rule we surely had to violate,
And then, with clever planning, place the blame
On someone else's doorstep! It was great
To point accusing fingers and cry "shame!"
We went to school and learned to read and write.
We grew and learned to drive the family car.
And when we learned to stay up late at night
Then we knew more than anyone, by far!
Our parents were still useful, but too bad
They didn't realize that times had changed.
We really knew it all; we thought we had
The answers; and our young ambitions ranged
Around the earth and off to outer space!
Bring on your challenges! We're well prepared!
No matter what the crisis we must face
We'll meet it, and no effort will be spared!
We've made our contribution to the race.
We've been the hero, while the coward stared!

We've climbed each peak with which
    we've been confronted;
We've looked around for faster speeds to pace us!
Our daring has been sharp and never blunted,
We're ready now for anything to face us!
We've really done a great job, you and I!
Come what may, I'm well prepared! Aren't you?

If we all knew that each of us must die
Within the hour, *just what would we do?*

Of all the plays that William Shakespeare wrote
One has been outstanding through the years.
The Tragedy of Hamlet, Prince of Denmark
Has often had its audience in tears,
While taxing talents of the tried and true
As each performer took a different view
Of what made Hamlet act the way he did.
Seeing his late father, who was hid
From revelation to most other eyes
Caused most of those around him to surmise
That he was mad. Yet, with a favored few,
He had forewarned them that this he must do
To catch the quickening conscience of the king

And trap him to admission that the thing
Which caused his father's death was by his hand
That he might become ruler of the land.
As Hamlet wove his web so cunningly
He took some solace in soliloquy.
While making up his mind which way to go
Resolve would often wander to and fro;
To be, or not to be: that is the question:—
Whether 'tis nobler in the mind to suffer
The slings and arrows of outrageous fortune,
Or to take arms against a sea of troubles,
And by opposing end them?—To die,—to sleep,
No more:—and, by a sleep, to say we end
The heart-ache, and the thousand natural shocks
That flesh is heir to,—'tis a consummation
Devoutly to be wished. To die,—to sleep:—
To sleep! perchance to dream:—ay, there's the rub;
For in that sleep of death what dreams may come,
When we have shuffled off this mortal coil,
Must give us pause. There's the respect,
That makes calamity of so long life:
For who would bear the whips and scorns of time,
The oppressor's wrong, the proud man's contumely,
The pangs of despised love, the law's delay,

The insolence of office, and the spurns
That patient merit of the unworthy takes,
When he himself might his quietus make
With a bare bodkin? who would fardels bear,
To grunt and sweat under a weary life,
But that the dread of something after death,—
The undiscovered country, from whose bourn
No traveller returns,—puzzles the will,
And makes us rather bear those ills we have
Than fly to others that we know not of?
Thus conscience does make cowards of us all;
And thus the native hue of resolution
Is sicklied o'er with the pale cast of thought;
And enterprises of great pitch and moment,
With this regard, their currents turn awry,
And lose the name of action.

Truly great
To read and understand those words today,
This very moment! It was not too late,
And thanks to God, that Martin Luther strode
Upon the waiting stage; he didn't wait
For someone else to do the job. The gate
Was open and he entered at God's call.
He made a forthright answer; what is more

He lived what he believed! He didn't stall!
With firmer faith than had been known before,
He made it possible for us today
To alter Shakespeare's words, and make them say:
"To be or not! *To be,* that is the Christian!"
It is far nobler in the heart to suffer
The slings and arrows of outrageous fortune,
And to take Christ against our sea of troubles
And by true loving end them. To die, to sleep;
No more; and by a sleep to say we end
The heartache and the thousand natural shocks
That flesh is heir to, 'tis a consummation
Devoutly to be *dreaded* by us all;
For did not Jesus come to bear the same?
Those selfsame slings and arrows He made His;
All of Him that was mortal took the shocks
That flesh is heir to, bore a consummation
Upon the cross, that all of us might know
When we have shuffled off this mortal coil
That even though each one of us must bear
The whips and scorns of time,
        the oppressor's wrong,
The pangs of despised love, the law's delay,
For every sleep there is awakening

Into eternal life. For us no dread
Of something after life which we must fear;
But faith and knowledge of the greater truth
That leads us to an even greater life
Where every empty promise we have made
Will be filled 'til our cup is running over
With love of God! True,
            conscience does make cowards
Of all who turn aside the truth of Jesus.
But for each one who leads the life of Christian
This world will open up each world beyond,
Until the very thought of our quietus
Will bring a firmer step into the future,
And by our very bearing, each who sees us
Will know that we are followers of Jesus!
So full my heart must be, and full of Thee,
If I shall truly live and truly be
The brother of my brother of my brother
Until I learn there always is another
Someone outside of me whom I must love
Just as I love myself! We cannot shove
Aside the sins, the hate, the petty greed
And justify them with the name of Need!
Better we look and not like what we see

Within ourselves. We cannot set man free
By granting him a pardon for his wrongs.
It is not ours to give—the right belongs
To God alone! He who created man
After His own image, surely can
Re-form him in His image once again,
Forgive his sins and hear his loud "amen"!

A simple word, "forgive"—whose real intention
Lies very close to us. The intervention
Of God in our behalf made the truth clear:
That all the man-made things we hold so dear
Are worthless when we realize the price
Already paid in our behalf by Christ!
When Christ says, "I forgive," He really says
For you I *give*—my life. I for you—give,
I truly die that you may truly live!

Well, now that we're forgiven, what about
Reform? Or does forgiveness cancel out
Each and every debt we might be owing
To all our fellow men, none of them knowing
If we shall ever try to pay the debt?
Of course we'll pay! In full! You wanna bet?

There isn't any more convenient phrase
For one who owes a debt before he dies
But manages to die before he pays
Than: "He lies here who swore he'd pay! He lies!"

If we all knew that each of us must die
Within the hour, just what would we do?
Perhaps at such a time, what we should do
Would be to ask ourselves "What have we done?"
Where were we false, and where have we been **true?**
Must we admit our constant search for fun
Filled every hour, every fleeting minute
'Til every job my Saviour had for me
I looked to see if there was pleasure in it
Before I said "Lord, here I am, send me!"

It seems to me the best thing for us all
Would be to live our lives each passing day
In such real love and truth that when the call
Rings out for us that we must go the way
All nature must, we'll proudly say, "I come"
And go because we have the means of grace,
Knowing that where we once saw through a glass
Darkly, we shall now see face to face;

Knowing that where we once knew in part
We'll know as we are known in God's own heart!

It must be clear to each of us today
No matter what our job or situation
To be prepared to take it, come what may,
Requires at least a partial reformation
Within our lives. The matter of degree
Will vary quite a bit undoubtedly.
But just as God formed us, we must re-form
As close to His own image as we can.
We have the wherewithal to be reborn
In Jesus Christ, who gives to every man
The way to learn to live, to learn to pray
For all the love of God and all His power
To heal, to teach, to love—and to obey
Whatever call may come at any hour!

What sort of call do you think God will give
To you and me? And do you think we'll know
The call has come from God? Or will we live
Such blinded lives that we may never grow
Quite tall enough to see above the crowd
That cries for Jesus' blood upon the cross,

And when we're challenged testify aloud
"Who, me? I never knew the man!" What loss
Of human life has ever known such price?

When Jesus knew He was about to die,
What did He do? Did He take friends' advice
To flee Jerusalem? And did He try
To comfort His disciples with the thought
That He would hide behind them and go free,
That they would see that He would not be caught?
Is that what Jesus wanted? Liberty?
Of course He did! And so do you and I!
But Jesus knew that freedom had its price:
To live for you and me, and then to die
Upon the cross, a loving sacrifice!

What gives the promise of a resurrection
To all who heed God's call? *For we are called*
To rid our petty lives of all infection
From sin! There is no time to sit enthralled
Upon the sidelines! This call is for you!
Such messages have a most familiar ring—
A message that is common all day through
In offices and homes, and it may bring
Some news of someone very near and dear.

You know the way the message goes—"Your wife
Just called. Please call her back. Mr. Revere
Will meet you at the station. Dr. Strife
Called up—he has the X rays of your teeth.
You'll need a lot of work done right away.
They look all right outside, but underneath
The pictures show a lot of new decay!
And by the way, God called." "What did He say?"
"Oh, nothing much; He just said 'Follow me'!"
You say it's nothing much? That simple phrase
Contains the formula, the recipe
For witnessing for Christ, the way to raise
The hopes of every Christian on this earth!
What will we do? What will our answer be?
The challenge has been with us since our birth.
Will we now answer, "Here I am! Send me!"
Use me! Use my head, my hands, my heart!
I'll put aside all else and do Thy will!
I'm here and ready, God! When do I start?
And God is apt to say to us, "Be still
And know that I am God!"
                              In the beginning
God made heaven and earth, and it was good!
He made us in His image, gave us food.
To show our gratitude we started sinning!

39

That's why, you see, we must be born again,
And why it's first important that we die
The death that purifies our lives—and then
We'll have our resurrection, you and I,
To live and love in every human heart;
To follow Jesus everywhere He wills;
To place our hand in His and never part;
To share the deep discouragement that fills
His heart for everyone who would deny Him;
To learn to say to all who would pass by Him:
"Before you turn your back, why don't you try
        Him?"
For each of us there's Jesus Christ to turn to.
For each, a better life that we can yearn to.
For each of us, a brother who will need us;
For each, a loving Father who will feed us.
For each of us, a sacrifice that frees us;
For each, at least one chance to die for Jesus.
For each of us, the opportunity
To light the way with love that all may see!
So keep your heads up high, your wits about you.
Walk tall, the way a Christian witness should!
You may doubt God, but God will never doubt *you;*
He'll see His image, and He'll call it good!

payable on demand

How do I love thee? Let me count the ways:
I love thee to the depth and breadth and height
My soul can reach, when feeling out of sight
For the ends of Being and ideal Grace.
I love thee to the level of everyday's
Most quiet need, by sun and candle-light.
I love thee freely, as men strive for Right;
I love thee purely, as they turn from Praise.
I love thee with the passion put to use
In my old griefs, and with my childhood's faith.
I love thee with a love I seemed to lose
With my lost saints,—I love thee with the breath,
Smiles, tears, of all my life!—and, if God choose,
I shall but love thee better after death.

Elizabeth Barrett Browning wrote those lines
Describing a love that would not let her go,
Singing a song of heart that made her so
Conscious of the ultimate, the eternal

Goal of all mankind, she could no longer
Keep it to herself, but, as a flower
Buds until it bursts, she chose the hour
In which to break the bonds that bound her soul
And pour her own peculiar balm of Gilead
Upon the world of man's sore troubled head.
Why have they lived, these lines of a mere mortal?
I'd like to try my best to tell you why!
Others have used their brightest shining phrases
To speak of love, all claiming love is grand!
Pat Boone sings of love letters in the sand.
Elvis Presley says he's all shook up!
Both pleasantries and banalities contrive
To keep all sorts of love affairs alive!
Write of the moon and June, sing of the stars;
Speak of a never-ending purple passion.
Swear by initials carved in yonder tree.
Pledge with a ring on left hand, finger four,
That yours is a love to last forevermore!
And who knows? Some may be right,
       some others wrong.
Sometimes some learn to sing another song!

But such was not the case with Mrs. Browning.

She spoke her love the way the Bible urges
When God asks us to work within His Kingdom.
A simple phrase, four very simple words,
Words of one syllable each, and yet you'll find
It threads its way throughout both testaments.
The simple words are these—
        "with the whole heart."

With God, halfheartedness will never do.
Christ gave "with the whole heart"
        that we might live!
Do we dare offer Him a half-a-heart?
I think you'll agree the answer must be "No."
Here, above all, must be a *quid pro quo!*
Half-hearts must live and thrive upon half-truths,
And here again we have an absolute
That cannot be cut down or qualified.
Oh, I know full well the poet and composer
Have tried to make of truth a partial thing,
Have tried to make of the resulting lie
A little thing, scarce worthy of our notice
And whiter than the pure and driven snow!
"Little white lies," they're called,
        and we are quick

To latch upon them as a means of grace
Among our fellow men if not with God.
But God is Truth, and Truth is God! Now try
Your level best to cut and qualify
God to the stature of a small white lie!

They tell a story you've most likely heard
Of three men bending truth to fit the word.
Three Navy men they were, all officers,
Who loved to pass the hours playing poker,
A habit which their Captain frowned upon!
He had forbidden them to play in quarters.
But one fine day he chanced to come upon
The three of them just after they had finished
Playing in full defiance of his order.
His temper in full-steam, he turned to one
And barked at him, "Have you been playing
      poker?"
Our young officer hemmed and hawed a bit
And finally blurted out, "No, Sir! Not I!"
The Captain turned his glare upon the second,
And sternly said, "Have you been playing poker?"
Our number two man seemed to have less trouble.
His "No, Sir!" came out clear and clean and crisp.

Both having denied that they'd been playing poker
The Captain trained his gaze on number three.
"And what about you? Have you been playing
        poker?"
Back came the swift rejoinder, "What, alone?"

Yes, God is Truth, and God is also Love;
So let us paraphrase a little bit
Where Paul reminds us all that, though we speak
With tongues of men and angels, and have not love,
Or—have not God, might just as well be said—
If we lack love—or God—we are become
As noisy, sounding brass or tinkling cymbal.
I'm sure that, if you think along with me,
You'll realize how beautifully Paul put it.
Sounding brass is merely brassy sound,
Noise, if you will, with no significance.
A cymbal, also brassy, can be said
To be the very opposite of Tinkle.
Without God or without Love we lack
Ability to make our presence known.
We lack the guiding principle of life
Which makes our every move significant.
How simple it is to be a vegetable!

The title of this talk with you might be
"Payable on Demand," and it may seem
That thus far I have done some poor connecting
Between the title and the things I've said.
Blank verse is quite a fascinating medium
In which to do a bit of sermonizing.
But still its use can never justify
The loss of theme and thought within its rhythms.
So please forgive! Connection coming up!
And high time, too, some of you may well say,
It's far too warm for wandering this way!
So be it!
       Look around you in this place!
Is yours a group which you consider friendly?
Are you quite happy here? And is it active,
This happiness of yours, or mere contentment,
Mere satisfaction with the *status quo?*
I'm sure that on some past Communion Sunday
When many joined our church, we stayed for coffee
And went through all the motions of a welcome,
And—then what? Did it stop right then and there?
Did we feel the church required a duty of us?
Did we feel that we'd discharged it rather well?
After all, we said "Hello" and "Welcome"—

What more was there to do? We'd gladly have them
To dinner once or twice, that is, if we
Could find the proper opportunity!

I wonder what would happen if, one day,
One Communion, Jesus Christ should pass this way
And, noticing the crowd, should happen in
And hear us all confess our every sin
To clear our conscience, that we might be able
To gather once again around the table
And hear the minister ministering in His name
Pronounce those wondrous words, the very same
Which He repeated once to His disciples.
And as he called the new members to rise
And come forward, suppose our own Lord Jesus
Stepped from a pew, walked forward with the rest!
And let's assume we *knew* that He was Jesus!
How would we welcome Him? Would we say
        "Welcome!
My name is Smith (or Jones, or Peterson).
I've been a member here for quite a while,
I'm sure that you'll be very happy here.
How do you like your coffee? Cream and sugar?
Let me know if there's anything I can do!"

The promissory note! I knew we'd get to it!
Payable on demand! "Just let me know
If there's anything I can do!" Did we say that?
And in this way we'd greet
        our Lord and Saviour?
Or give Him invitations by the score
And hope that we had issued just one more
Than any of the others. Would we boast
Of special meals prepared, how good the roast
The night He came to our house? Or would we
Brag of well-established intimacy:
"Why, just the other day, I said, J.C.!——"
Name dropping as we do!—Don't be offended,
No sacrilegious insult was intended.
I just was bent on wondering aloud
How Jesus would have mingled in our crowd!
Would any of us, recognizing Him,
Have bowed the knee, or washed His feet, or kissed
The hem of any garb He might be wearing?
And would we have thought it
        far beneath our bearing
To treat *just any other* new member so?

I wonder why? Remember when Jesus said:

48

"I was an hungred, and ye gave me meat;
I was thirsty, and ye gave me drink;
I was a stranger, and ye took me in;
I was naked, and ye gave me clothes;
I was sick, and ye visited me;
I was in prison, and ye came unto me!"
Would not we, as did the disciples, ask of Him:
"Lord, when saw we thee an hungred and fed thee?
Or thirsty and gave thee aught to drink?
When saw we thee a stranger and took thee in?
Or when saw we thee naked and clothed thee?
When saw we thee sick and visited thee?
Or in prison and came unto thee?"
Then the *King* shall answer and say to us:
"Verily, verily I say unto you,
Inasmuch as ye have done it unto *one*
Of the least of these my brethren, ye have done it
Unto me!"
      So let it be with friendship!
For Jesus, when He hung upon the cross,
Owed no one anything, there was no loss
To anyone, there were no creditors;
And yet He made Himself the greatest debtor
The world has ever known! He signed the note.

With His own strong and loving nail-pierced hand
He wrote across it, "Payable on Demand!"

And so we are taught from early infancy
To make demands on Him. And do we do it!
We cash that note a thousand times with ease,
Even demanding interest when we please!

On some Communion Sunday, past or future,
We stood or will stand arm in arm with Jesus,
For every other one who stands there with us
Will be the same as our beloved Saviour.
We proudly answer "Yes" when we are asked
To dedicate our lives to Jesus Christ.
We gladly sign the promissory note,
But—do we write with firm and eager hand
Above our signature—Payable on Demand?
There's just one way I know of to determine
And that's to make demands upon each other.
Friendship and Love are very like a muscle,
They must be used or they will atrophy.
So use each other's friendship, love and truth,
And, in the words of Shakespeare, if you do
Then it must follow as the night the day

Thou canst not then be false to any man!
Serve and love each other, on demand!
Help and aid each other, on demand!
Never forget that God created man
After His own image, and God is Love—
So man is Love, and it behooves us all
To keep ourselves so very bright and shining
That all around may see themselves in us!
If we do this for one of the least of these,
The day will come when we'll drop to our knees
In gratitude, when someone looking deep
Within our souls, will see the face of Jesus;
And then we'll know the priceless, matchless thrill
Of knowing that, on demand, we paid the bill!
For in the very paying lies the food
On which the spirit feeds and starts to grow
To knowledge every one of us may know
And realize again that God is good!
That God is Truth and Love! And everyone
Who grows in Him will realize by teaching
The farthest goals are well within our reaching!

All of us remember Jesus said,
"Suffer the little children to come to me!"

For those who teach, a paraphrase might be,
"Suffer *with* little children to come to me!"

The months ahead are filled to overflowing
With challenges we can't anticipate;
But we can make demands on God, well knowing
His promise will be kept. Let's consecrate
Each hour that we live to teach by giving
The truth and love God gives each for his own.
Thus shall we grow, and learn the art of living,
And, what is more, we'll never be alone!

What a wondrous, peaceful planet this would be
If we could look around ourselves and see
Each total stranger as another friend,
That we might know and love him, to the end
That we might say, as in our opening phrase,
"How do I love thee? Let me count the ways!"

what price resurrection?

There never was a time in all of time
Since History began when all was new
That cried out more for braver ones to climb
The topless towers of love for me and you
Than now! Not just the "now" we know today,
The "now" we sometimes call "our generation"—
Each now from long ago and far away,
The ever-present "present" of each nation
That for its time held forth upon the stage
And played a leading role of war or peace
Writing with strong, firm hand upon a page
Of the World's Book these words,
        "All wars must cease!"
You've heard it? Sure you have! And so have I!
And each time it was uttered it was done
With best of all intentions—with a cry
Of "Peace! We must have peace for everyone!"

What can bring "peace on earth, good will to men"?
Is there some secret formula we can try?
Is there some way to touch men's hearts again?
Are we too busy probing through the sky
To take the time to try to ascertain
Just what we want of life? —To make it plain
No matter what we want we'll not achieve it
Until we find the truth and then believe it!
The selfsame set of standards, once applied,
Will make one person stand up for the right,
Yet make another person run and hide,
And still another try with all his might
To blow both hot and cold, and justify it
In such a way that other fools may try it!

There was a Man who walked this very earth
Comparatively briefly as such things
Are measured nowadays, who from His birth
Was destined to be called the King of kings,
And destined to be hammered to a cross
By frightened men who watched until He died!
Yet mankind's greatest gain came from this loss;
And there were those who cheered—
        and those who cried!

Christ Jesus said we must be born again
If we would taste the fullest fruits of life
Both now and after death. So many men
Believe such rebirth only comes from strife;
Like birth, each rebirth has its share of pain—
That only through some suffering can we gain
Access to all the promise of the cross
Wherein the richest gain may grow from loss!
Not to a precious few, but to all men
God's gift was given! Tiny Bethlehem
Knows what it is each year to shine again
With starlight for the shepherds, for to them
Was sung a loud Te Deum, and they stood
In awesome silence through the final sound;
And at the manger made of rough-hewn wood
Where even wondering Wise Men gathered 'round,
They marveled that this tiny baby boy
Could bring to *all* their first true taste of joy!

I find it hard to trust my mind when thinking
That some force sent a *few* into this world
Booted and set to ride, already drinking
To victory, new battle flags unfurled—
And millions meekly doing as they're bidden,

All saddled and all bridled to be ridden!
I simply can't believe it, for I know
That each and every one of us may see
The selfsame truths that move men to and fro
Across the earth and to eternity!
So make your own decision what you'll be—
A son of God, or Mammon's strong defense!
But only with the former will you see
Those stars which help to make the fog less dense!
We must be born again! It seems quite clear
That each of us must give up many things
That in our lives we've learned to hold so dear;
For only a new scale of values brings
That keener vision which enables man
To see beyond his nose and find his place
Within our Heavenly Father's perfect plan
Which holds each one within His warm embrace.

Surely to be born again contains
No mystery—it happens every day
Within our universe. The very grains
Of sand the oceans seem to throw away
Only to claim again, are changed each time
In size and shape and re-appear quite new.

And every star, before it starts its climb
Seems to renew its light. John Milton knew
Some secrets of the heavens when he wrote
This excerpt from "Lycidas" which I quote:
So sinks the day-star in the ocean bed,
And yet anon repairs his drooping head,
And tricks his beams, and with new-spangled ore
Flames in the forehead of the morning sky.

Let us combine that greatest gift of all—
Jesus' resurrection from the grave—
With what we must do, if we are to call
Upon the only power that can save
Mankind from self-destruction. For you see
Rebirth and resurrection are the same—
Their meaning is the same for you and me—
Each merely has a different sounding name.

When Christ was resurrected from the dead,
Bearing the marks of thorns upon His head,
Bearing the wounds in side and foot and hand,
Knowing that those who loved would understand,
He had been born again! He who was human
And also God, had carried out His plan!

Born once from deep within the womb of woman
Reborn from deep within the tomb of man!

Each day contains its share of crucifixion—
Each day contains its chances for rebirth!
Each day contains its share of fact and fiction—
Each day contains its chance for waste or worth!
Each hour knows its part in any story;
Each minute knows the value of a tear;
Each second ticks its way on paths of glory;
Each moment knows the tragedy of fear!
But somewhere in each corner of creation
And somewhere in the soul of every man
There lives that part of God's imagination
That makes us part of God's eternal plan!
It's easier to make an illustration
Far more convincing, even when you rhyme
By making up your facts and information.
So here's a story: Once upon a time
In World War II there was a little town
In Western Germany; and one big raid
By air had blown its every building down.
Yet not one of its people was afraid.
When our G.I.'s came marching through its streets,

Or what was left of them, they knew the part
Which they must play, and as one stranger greets
Another stranger, deep within its heart
That town began interpreting the role
Of building for a new place in the sun
And filling in the last exploded hole
Which lingered when the last air raid was done.
One G.I. from the U.S. was appalled
That he had had a hand in devastating
This little man-made village. He recalled
His own home when his father was creating
Along with many others in the town
The first rough plans to build a village square
With proper public buildings, and to crown
The biggest of these buildings with a pair
Of flagpoles by all odds the very tallest
That memory of man had ever known.
And then they searched and found the very
      smallest
Inhabitant and sent him out alone
Across the fragrant fields, until he found
The last point where the flags could still be seen
When standing on his tiptoes on the ground;
And they declared that all the land between

Would soon be filled with churches,
          homes and schools,
And anyone who wanted to could be
A part of this great promise! Only fools
Would dare deny such opportunity!
Then he recalled the growth which followed after—
The careful planning, how the highways came
And brought more people. He recalled the laughter
At some suggestions when they changed the name
Of their once tiny town, which now achieved
The status of a city, and the pride
Of knowing that because a few believed
A city had been built!
                    But *here* one died!
One quiet little village, with its people
The only things still standing on its ground,
Except the barest outline of a steeple
Proclaiming to the world for miles around
That God had once been here, and would again
Walk softly through this ruined German place
And move out from within the hearts of men
To put a smile on every human face!

Our G.I. looked—and thought—and then decided

That when the world was once again at peace
And men and women once again were guided
By thoughts of common good—when the increase
Of ways to wipe away the face of man
From every corner of his precious earth
Should so destroy and warp his every plan
For life that death might seize him at his birth—
At such a time, and through sheer desperation
When cold war was the order of the day
And brought a troubled peace to every nation—
Then he resolved to come again this way
And help to clear the rubble from this town,
That once again the fields might feel the plow
And grass might grow again, while up and down
The streets and lanes which were deserted now
Would rise again new homes and happy people,
And over all, the brand-new church's steeple!

This he resolved to do! And to his credit
He tried his best to bring it all about
Exactly as he meant it when he said it!
So, three or four years later, he set out
With all the money he could save or borrow
To buy the first essentials which were needed

To make the buried town forget its sorrow
And rise again! When all the fields were seeded
And corn and wheat and vegetables were growing
And hunger had completely disappeared
And happy builders lived each full day, knowing
That each new day held nothing to be feared,
He knew that little town would grow so fast
That, like his own, it soon might be a city
And push beyond the troubles of its past
To happiness!

             It rather seems a pity
His idea was so strong that he forgot
The power God gives all He may create
To call upon divinity, and not
To entertain destruction—not to wait
For help to come from distant points outside
But catch a breath, and roll the stones away
From all the rubble where the town had died
That it might live again and face the day
Of new faith and new life!

               And so our friend
Was startled when he came upon the place
Where he had seen the brave town meet its end
To see it turn a bright and brand-new face

To welcome him! He couldn't find a scar!
New homes and buildings stood on shining streets
Exactly as before! And near and far
The busy sound of happiness which greets
The ears of all who listen and have eyes
To see a town so scorn its own demise
That it could rise again, and point with pride
At its new life, as if it never died!

How often must we struggle with the thought
That Jesus Christ once died that you and I
Might live again, and with His blood He bought
Our right to know that as each day goes by
The faith and hope and love with which He came
Is there for us to have if we but ask!
Just ask! The invitation is the same
To every generation! And the task
That seems so very difficult to do
Will know divine mind's guidance and will seem
So simple and so easy to see through!
Just ask! And every door of every dream
That looks to all men loving every neighbor
Will open on a bright new world of peace;
And God will know that His unceasing labor

Has brought about that time when war shall cease!

When "Praise the Lord and pass the ammunition"
Became a well-known song of World War Two,
It pointed up again man's inhibition
At putting all his trust in God. How few
Of all the men the world has ever known
Were able to accomplish such a trust;
And those who did it, learned to walk alone
Among their doubting friends! And yet we must
Look deep within ourselves—cast out the dead
And dying thoughts that lead but to the grave—
Take leadership and bravely march ahead
Into each day's new dawn, if we would save
Mankind, and make of every man a friend
Facing the future filled with hope and love,
Facing a life of truth that knows no end—
Facing a world of trust in God above!

64